Intestinal Cleanse and Reconstruction

The Most Powerful Internal Detoxification Program

Nekoterran

From the Author:

I want to thank you and congratulate you for purchasing the book *Intestinal Cleanse and Reconstruction: The Most Powerful Internal Detoxification Program.*

This program contains proven steps and strategies on how to cleanse the small and large intestines and to reconstruct the delicate intestinal lining.

Deep internal cleansing programs available on the marketplace take months to clean out the mucoid plaque in the bowels. Most of these programs are missing 50% of information and deliver only marginal results.

In this program, you will learn unmatched wisdom on how to clean out mucoid plaque, fungal overgrowth, parasites, and unfriendly bacteria in a matter of days.

If you have been searching for a deep internal cleanse that delivers maximum results...your search has just ended.

Thanks again for purchasing this book. I hope you not only read but take action on the information as well.

CONTENTS:

If you enjoy this book do consider leaving a review…

www.nekoterran.com/advice

Read Together With:

Basic Bodybuilding

✓ What builds muscles.

✓ What causes muscle mass deterioration.

✓ What causes body fat.

✓ How to burn body fat.

✓ How to maintain muscle mass.

✓ How to maintain a fat-less physique.

✓ Choose only basic bodybuilding or basic weight loss.

Basic Weight Loss

- ✓ What tones/strengthens muscles.
- ✓ What causes muscle mass deterioration.
- ✓ What causes body fat.
- ✓ How to prevent body fat.
- ✓ How to burn existing body fat.
- ✓ How to maintain muscle mass.
- ✓ How to maintain a fat-less physique.
- ✓ Choose only basic bodybuilding or basic weight loss.

Introduction:

I am not a fitness instructor or a doctor, nor do I have a coaching license.

The information in this program is not tailored to replace your current diet or health regimen. This program has not been evaluated by the AFAA, Medical Fitness Association, American Sports and Fitness Association, FDA, IDEA Health & Fitness Association or any other health association.

All the information you will learn is based on direct experience and experimentation on myself, my bodybuilding peers, fitness enthusiasts and the average out-of-shape individual who also achieved outstanding results.

However, it is possible that the techniques outlined have some measure of risk, like everything in this world. You have to use common sense and consult with your physician if necessary prior to a cleanse and dietary principles. You, the reader alone, is the only one responsible for the methods outlined in this program.

What is in this program?

This program is a step-by-step guide to cleanse the small and large intestines and reconstruct the intestinal wall lining. If you desire to know what causes mucoid plaque buildup, excess body fat, alkaline body temperatures, and everything to stay in optimal shape→ **all this information is covered in my other programs:**

1. *How to Burn Body Fat Completely and Maintain a Slim Physique Permanently*

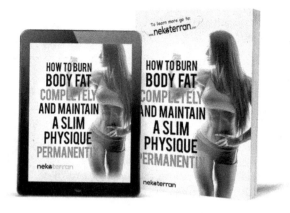

2. *How to Build More Muscle than Ever Before and Maintain Muscle Mass Permanently*

Choose only **one** program – Weight Loss or Bodybuilding

One program focuses on weight loss and the other on bodybuilding, but the health/nutritional information in the two separate titles are basically the same. The only differences would be the workout section and supplementation. Throughout this short read are lists of natural herbs and supplements required to successfully clean out and repair the intestines for peak performance.

Intestinal cleansing and reconstruction is divided into 3 steps.

1. Clean out excess mucoid plaque buildup.

2. Transplant friendly bacteria.

3. Reconstruct the bowel lining to cure leaky gut syndrome.

Note: Be warned…deep internal cleansing is a hard process. A deep internal detox is far more challenging than dieting or exercise alone. **But if you choose to follow through with the guidelines in these pages, your health, fitness, body and every area of your life will improve to new heights you won't have experienced.** Deep tissue cleansing requires time, patience, persistence and a disciplined effort that may be too much to handle for some. Each cleanse will last several days and the reconstruction phase will take weeks.

Your body will feel light, free, and burst with energy knowing that the useless gunk has been expelled from your system.

Losing weight, staying lean and building muscle mass will become a more pleasurable process, and you will obtain superior results.

Signs of toxic buildup in the bowels

There is an old saying, "Death begins in the colon." Believe it or not, most diseases, cancers and deaths happen due to sluggish bowels. In most cases, the cause of all the trouble is due to the re-absorption of toxicity buildup, unfriendly bacteria and rotting foods.

Signs of toxic overload:

- Low energy
- Irritability, mood swings
- Constipation
- Bloating
- Gas
- Headaches
- Fatigue
- Aches and pains
- Nausea
- Belly fat (hard to lose)
- Skin breakouts

Once all the necessary nutrition has been absorbed, the undesired waste must be removed.

What happens if the bowels don't function up to par?

The 3 major adversities are:

1. Hardened fecal matter in the bowels will disrupt digestion.

2. Due to the hardened fecal matter (mucus or mucoid plaque), only 10% - 20% of proper (healthy) nutrients can be absorbed. 80% - 90% of nutrients go to waste.

3. Bowel movement will slow down polluting the internal system. Digested foods can get stuck in the mucoid plaque.

If the colon is backed up, or if digestion is poor or eliminates only portions of waste, then the body will struggle to lose weight and build muscle, experience bloating, pollution, constipation and disease.

Hardened fecal matter accommodates the perfect home for fungi, parasites and unfriendly bacteria to overwhelm over time.

What is mucoid plaque/fecal matter?

Do an image search on mucoid plaque, bowel mucus, mucus rope and observe what comes up. More than 90% of diseases are diet and internal pollution related. The list would go on and on with alallhe internal and external damage that unhealthy bowels causes.

In this program, you will learn how to eliminate the intestinal mucoid plaque, parasites, unfriendly bacteria, fungi and parasite eggs effectively. Eliminating intestinal gunk is insufficient. The second half of the program consists of reconstructing the small and large intestines to be healthy and to flourish with friendly bacteria and to create a clean and healthy environment within…**long-term**.

There are hundreds of internal cleansing programs available. Most programs can take up to months or years to complete. Even then, the majority of the mucoid plaque, parasites, and fungal overgrowth will only be marginally cleaned out. In this program, you will learn how to dispose of all, if not 90%+, of the mucoid plaque in a matter of days. Not only to purge the bowels, but to reconstruct the frail intestinal lining (what is missing from most internal cleansing programs) and to transplant friendly bacteria to flourish for long periods of time. Yes, more than one cleanse is necessary…and yes, this will be a process...but you will experience results after just one cleanse.

Note: Areas to keep in mind:

a) Cleaning out is only half the battle.

b) The damaged intestinal walls must be addressed to eliminate outdated food quickly for a new digestive cycle to commence.

c) Cleansing for more than 10 days can weaken the internal organs.

d) The intestines and internal organs must be strengthened and reconstructed immediately following a cleanse.

e) **Important:** Fiber and laxatives are necessary during a fast. If old waste or mucoid plaque is not expelled from the system during the cleansing phase, it will remain sitting inside, rotting, congesting and polluting the system once you return to eating solid foods.

f) After the completion of a cleanse, transplanting friendly bacteria recolonizes the bowels with good bacteria for optimal absorption.

The step-by-step process is structured in such a way that none of the steps can be skipped or ignored.

Nothing in this program is theory or speculative. All the steps have been tested and proven to be highly effective.

Why is cleansing the intestines and reconstructing the intestinal walls necessary?

Pathways of elimination:

Comparable to the analogy of a drainage system, if the sewers become backed up or packed with sewage, the drainage tubes/pipelines will clog, leading to petrification of old waste and compromising the entire drainage system. Sooner or later, the gutter will spill over, causing the outside to become a sewer too. This is literally what happens to the body.

Basics:

The entire human body is made up of a compact system of tubes. The veins, bowels, muscles, and individual cells are a bunch of tubes. If the tubes become congested or blocked, toxicity will build up over time.

The body expels waste through the bowels, kidneys, skin and lungs. Just like the sewer system analogy, if the bowels (primary pathway of elimination) become overloaded, the body is forced to pack away fat tissue.

If the bowels become clogged for long periods of time, the waste expels through skin and lungs (secondary pathways of elimination).

What does this mean?

Old waste must be eliminated from the system quickly.

What do the small and large intestines (bowels and colon) have to do with health, fitness, weight loss or bodybuilding?

Imagine carrying around 20 lb – 40 lb (10 kg – 20 kg) of slime or gunk inside your bowels. The gunk is clogging, irritating, and creating a breeding home for parasites, fungal overgrowth, and unfriendly bacteria to live and feed on.

Decades and decades of eating the wrong incompatible foods has led to kilos (pounds upon pounds) of built up/hardened mucoid plaque and fecal matter in the intestinal walls. Furthermore, mucoid plaque clogs the entire system from expelling waste, slowing down the digestive process and bowel movements. This eventually leads to disease. As abundant as 10 – 20 kilos or 20 – 40 pounds of mucoid plaque can accumulate in the intestines.

The average adult has proven by autopsies to have up to 9 inches in diameter of mucoid plaque buildup, stuck in the bowel's interior walls. Encrusted onto the bowel walls for years, the plaque allows passage for only a thin pencil.

Once the plaque accumulates, all the food, healthy or otherwise, gets stuck on the plaque, sitting in the bowels for days if not for weeks without expulsion.

The bowels are one of the primary channels of elimination.

What does the intestines and bowel movements have to do with health, fitness, weight loss and bodybuilding?

The bowels have EVERYTHING to with health, fitness, weight loss and bodybuilding.

Like the analogy of a dishwashing machine from my weight loss and bodybuilding books... once a set of dishes has completed a cleaning session, the old set (washed dishes) must be removed, and a new set (more dirty dishes) inserted, to begin a new washing cycle.

How do you know if you need an internal detox?

If you don't have a bowel movement first thing in the morning, and 40 minutes after every large meal, you are chronically constipated!

A cleanse is only half the battle. Cleaning out (cleansing) the intestines alone will leave the bowels weakened and open to infections. After years and years of consuming incompatible foods, fungal overgrowth, parasites, and acidity from white flour, coffee, processed and refined grains have damaged the intestinal walls causing leaky gut syndrome. The bowel lining can be punctured by hundreds if not thousands of holes. Food particles can leak out the intestines polluting the blood causing major damage to the liver, gallbladder and the surrounding organs.

Hard to believe? The next time you go number #2, examine your stools (poop).

Are your stools large in circumference, 1-inch in diameter, and shaped like a banana?

After the completion of the program, mucoid plaque, parasites and leaky gut will be all gone.

Symptoms of leaky gut:

- Digestive Issues: gas, bloating, diarrhea or irritable bowel syndrome
- Food Sensitivities: food allergies, food intolerance
- Inflammatory Bowel Disease
- Autoimmune Disease: lupus, psoriasis, celiac disease
- Thyroid Problems
- Malabsorption
- Inflammatory Skin Conditions
- Mood Issues
- Seasonal Allergies

By cleansing and reconstructing the intestines, the above symptoms will be eradicated.

Why does mucoid plaque accumulate?

Comparable to the idea of snot forming inside the nostrils when someone catches a cold, the body excretes mucus to surround foods that are poisonous to protect the organs. The mucus-coated food is expelled out the bowels. If large doses of incompatible/wrong/poisonous foods are consumed for prolonged periods of time, mucus cannot excrete fast enough, or too much mucus is excreted leading to excess buildup of rock-hardened mucoid plaque that affixes to the intestinal walls. The bowel walls will be forced to bulge like balloons to accommodate the excess mucoid plaque buildup; in medical terms, this is called diverticulosis.

Do you know why all small children under the age of 8 have perfectly clear skin and their breath smells fresh?

The reason is because they haven't had enough time to damage their liver, intestines and gallbladder. The feces or poop of small children is large in circumference of 1.5 inches or bigger (4 cm–5 cm). An adult over the age of 18 is fortunate if their feces is large enough to be ½ - ¾ of an inch (2 cm) in circumference. Excess mucoid plaque buildup for years allows less than ½ inch (2 cm) diameter of digested food to pass out, constipating and clogging the entire system.

Friendly bacteria or probiotics flourish in healthy intestines. Unfriendly bacteria, fungal overgrowth, and parasites cannot survive in an alkaline environment fully colonized by friendly bacteria. **Once the gunk has been cleaned out, absorption and digestion will improve considerably.**

Health experts' argument:

A number of health experts dispute that the colon/bowel/intestinal/internal cleansing can backfire because a deep internal detox wipes out friendly bacteria→ which is absolutely true!

They are convinced that the human's internal organs are capable of repairing, and able to self-nurture a healthy habitat on its own.

If you suffered a deep cut in the midsection, suffering from large amounts of internal and external bleeding, would you head to the hospital or allow the bleeding to stop over time and the wound to heal naturally?

The answer is obvious.

Destroying and expelling out the mucoid plaque will wipe out all the friendly probiotics, unfriendly bacteria, fungi, parasites, old foods, new foods, everything. Once the insides have been detoxified, the bowels are open wide to new infections.

Immediately following the detox, the gut must be re-colonized and repaired.

If anyone says that deep internal cleansing is not necessary, they are misinformed on how the human body works.

How is mucoid plaque cleaned out completely, subtle intestinal walls patched, and finally fully re-colonized by friendly bacteria?

Intestinal cleansing and reconstruction is divided into 3 steps.

1. Break down and clean out mucoid plaque buildup.

2. Transplant friendly bacteria (during and after a cleanse).

3. Reconstruct the bowel lining to cure leaky gut syndrome.

Steps 2 and 3 can and must be done together at the same time.

Cleansing and reconstructing the intestines is more challenging than it sounds. A lot of stress will be put upon the body forcing the release of toxins into the blood stream that would not normally be present. Rest assured, the rewards will outrank the physical and mental pressure times a million.

Some people who have never done any kind of deep tissue cleanse will have amassed large amounts of toxic buildup in their system. If this is your situation, you have to approach the detox more slowly. It is actually possible to poison yourself if your body releases more toxins than it is able to handle at any one time. If the cleansing reactions become too severe, you will have to slow down the cleanse or end the cleanse completely for a time.

If you are pregnant or under a lot of stress in school or work or with other heavy duties, it would be wise to put off cleansing until you're more relaxed or on vacation or break.

Facts about cleansing

Most colon/bowel/intestinal cleanses available in the marketplace only address step #1.

Furthermore, most cleanses are not powerful enough and do a poor job of expelling the mucoid plaque. If it cleans the plaque out at all, those programs could take months upon months of cleansing. Chronically cleansing the bowels without transplanting probiotics or reconstructing intestinal lining is dangerous. Cleansing alone will leave the internal organs weakened. Cleansing for long periods of time (over 10 days) without rest will also overly-weaken paralytic actions of the intestines. As you are beginning to learn, there are several areas to attack.

What used to take months upon months to preform and years to complete, no longer is the case. The cleansing guidelines in this program will clean out a large portion of the mucoid plaque in only a matter of days.

Note: If there's anything in this world to invest money in→ it is your health. Everything money can buy is actually very cheap because those items can always be replaced. But the things we got as standard equipment for free, like our body and health, can never be replaced.

The principles in this program are very powerful.

You might ask: But isn't everyone's body different?

Answer: Everyone's body, internal organs, digestion, elimination, and assimilation function *exactly the same*.

Let me make one thing absolutely clear from the start:

I am not interested in advertising supplements,

nor am I pushing anyone to buy herbs.

Some nutrients are just impossible to be consumed from foods alone.

The necessary herbs add up to $160 - $170.

The supplements listed in this program are all NATURAL and do not carry any harmful side effects whatsoever.

If you still cannot agree to spend at least $160 - $170 on the necessary supplements...**stop reading right now!** Because this program is not for you.

Internal detoxification means serious business.

And this program is only for the committed.

Before we go into HOW to cleanse, let's first cover WHEN to cleanse.

Have you ever noticed during the spring, people catch colds or experience flu-like symptoms?

These symptoms are actually cleansing reactions because spring is the time when nature designed mammals and humans for deep tissue cleansing. The best time to cleanse is during the spring. This is the time when the body will not be stressed externally, and you will achieve the best results. On the other hand, winter is the worst time to cleanse due to the heavy burden the cold weather puts on the body. Fall and summer are ok to cleanse, but spring is the ideal time.

DEEP INTERNAL DETOXIFICATION

Let's begin the cleanse.

The 3 steps to cleanse effectively:

a. **Raw fast.**

For the body to cleanse, just like there is digestion mode and exercise mode, the body has to be forced into cleanse mode. If there is a heavy demand on digestion (eating cooked food), the body won't go into cleanse mode. The only way to fully go into cleanse mode is by eating only raw vegetables and moderate quantities of fruits and drinking plenty of water and green drinks during the cleanse. If you eat any kind of cooked food during the raw fast, your body will be kicked out of cleanse mode.

b. **Add stimulants to break down hardened mucoid plaque.**

Some of these stimulants would include laxative herbs, herbs that break up the plaque, and digestive enzymes.

c. **Expel toxins from the large intestines effectively.**

Breaking up the mucoid plaque and toxins within the bowels is only the beginning. If the toxins and waste just sit in the bowels, they will be re-absorbed into the intestines. Bentonite clay is what latches on or grabs the mucoid plaque, and fiber will force or pull out any leftovers out of your body preventing re-absorption.

What to consume during the cleanse:

What are green drinks?

Green drink is another name for vegetable juice and grass juice.

Any non-starchy vegetables are great to juice with a pinch of lime or stevia to improve the taste.

How many lemons have to be squeezed for one drinking glass? 5-6 lemons or more.

The point is, by juicing vegetables, large quantities of vegetables that cannot possibly be consumed in solid form can be consumed in juice form. Never underestimate the power of juicing. A highly alkaline internal environment will boost energy and maintain a clean internal system.

Alkaline body pH levels, the internal environment established inside the intestines, is crucial for health, internal detoxification, weight loss, bodybuilding...everything! If you keep your vehicle (body) clean→ disease, body fat, loss of muscle, aging process (oxidation), mucoid plaque, parasites, molds, candida and fungal overgrowth cannot survive. Alkaline pH levels cannot be emphasized enough. And of course, a deep internal detoxification will go a long way in keeping the system clean.

Purchasing a quality blender can be a life-changing event. Juicing green drinks or juicing anything else and pretty much cooking overall will never be the same experience from this point onwards.

Most cheap/average blenders break down, burn out, and over-heat vegetable juices. As you will learn, if the vegetable juices are heated, enzymes within the raw plants will die.

Choose a blender of your choice.

FREE shipping.

Certified Reconditioned- 5300 $299

Personal- S30 $329

Legacy (food blender) - 5200 $449

Ascent Series A2300 $469

Some chain names that use Vitamix:

Starbucks, Beans Bins, Jamba Juice, Jugo Juice, Booster Juice, Lavazza Coffee, Tully's, Costa Coffee, Robeks, Maui Wowi Hawaiian Coffee & Smoothies, Smoothie King, Mr. Smoothie, Orange Julius, Tropical Smoothie Café, and the list goes on.

The next time you visit any coffee, juice, or smoothie chain store, sneak a peek at what blender they are using. I assure you that they will be using a Vitamix blender...and there is a reason for this.

The reason is because Vitamix blenders are of the highest quality, incomparable to any other blender in the marketplace.

The feature I like the most about the Vitamix blender is that the motor is extremely powerful and will never overheat the vegetable juices, keeping the enzymes alive. The only downside I can think of is that the motor is loud and heavy.

All the recipes available at the chain names can be replicated at home using the Vitamix blender. Even healthy alternatives for ice-cream, junk foods, chocolate shakes with stevia, sauces, dressings, and even soups can be made. Any kind of unhealthy food or sugar-packed junk food has a healthy substitute using a high-quality blender. Believe me, cooking will never be the same again.

To juice using a blender or juicer is the traditional way of juicing. This approach requires a high-quality blender and large amounts of vegetables, and it is extremely time consuming. Any green, leafy, non-starchy vegetable is ok to juice, including seaweed. This method is the best; however, the downside of using a juicer is that it can be expensive. If you are able to juice vegetables, that is the number one choice.

To force the body into cleansing mode, the digestive stress must be eliminated completely.

1. Pre-made vegetable juice:

    Sugar-free, green vegetable and grass juices. Vegetable juices are the most alkalizing fluids you can possibly ingest that do not require any effort to digest, and they are your ticket to getting into cleanse mode. The number 1 way to juice would be by using a high-quality blender. If a blender is not accessible, option number 2 would be to obtain fresh organic vegetable juices from a juice bar. All the leafy green vegetables are packed with enzymes that are vitally necessary to enhance cleansing.

2. Manually made vegetable juice:

   Anything and everything green + leafy + organic is super for juicing. Some options would include green lettuce, romaine lettuce, raw seaweed, cabbage, celery, spinach, Brussel sprouts, green onion, sprouts, arugula, celery, kale, Napa cabbage…. Be creative; anything green and leafy is an ideal choice.

The good news: There is a cheaper yet effective way to consume alkalizing vegetable drinks. And that is with green drink powder. Green drink powders would be the fast food replacement for juicing vegetables.

And if option 1 or 2 is unavailable, I would recommend using green powdered drinks. Here are my favorite green drink products.

All natural supplements are listed in:

www.nekoterran.com/supplements

Choose only one supplement from each category.

SUPER GREENS, #1 Green Veggie Superfood Powder, 8.5 oz **$24.95**

Amazing Grass Green Superfood, Original, Powder, 60 servings **$33.55**

Amazing Grass Green SuperFood ORAC, 100 Servings, 24.7 oz **$48.39**

Note: Fruits are very cleansing but are also high in fructose/natural sugar content. Excess sugar consumption spikes blood sugar levels and causes fungal overgrowth. Consume fruits in small quantities at a time, and eat fruits only in solid form. Avoid fruit juices except for adding some lime juice due to the high fructose content.

✓ I repeat…if cooked food is consumed during the cleanse, the body will be ousted of cleanse mode. Even cooked vegetables will force the body out from the detox. During the cleanse, eat and drink as many raw, green, leafy vegetables as possible. If you must have a hot drink, herbal tea is fine. Stay away from cow milk, soy milk, alcoholic beverages, nuts, seeds of any kind, bread and meats or eggs.

And of course, if you have read my other books, consuming coconut oil during cleansing will boost energy levels and will never kick the body out of cleansing mode. Taking coconut oil, flax oil and cod liver oil is most recommended. Whenever you feel hunger or lack energy, a few scoops of coconut oil will do. Stevia is also fine to add some flavor.

Listen to your body. Listening to our bodies is something we seldom do. Make your body your friend, not your enemy. Once your body begins to cleanse, you will feel flu-like symptoms, weak and very sick. Do not be alarmed! Assembled toxicity over years of consuming the wrong foods is suddenly being expelled all at once.

Note: It's possible to poison yourself if too much toxicity is released all at once. As long as you can handle the cleansing reactions, stay on the cleanse.

If the cleansing reactions are strong yet tolerable, that means you are on the right track. Be strong enough to resist the reactions.

However, if the cleansing reactions become too severe to the level you are unable to tolerate it, then end the cleanse all together, take a break for couple of days, and start over because your body is extremely toxic. The internal pollution has to be expelled sooner or later. Better sooner vs later.

---

2 Stages of Cleansing:

The cleanse is separated into two separate stages.

Stage 1 (2–4 days)

Stage 1 consists of raw cleansing foods + alkaline green drinks + cleansing herbs (breaks and destroys the mucoid plaque buildup) + bentonite clay and psyllium husk fiber. Eating large amounts of green vegetables, eating moderate amounts of fruits, and unlimited amounts of green drinks is necessary to go into cleanse mode on stage 1.

During stage 1, you will drink as many green drinks as possible and eat copious quantities of raw vegetables 2 to 3 times a day. Eat like any other meal, without any cooked food. Later, you will be adding cleansing herbs, bentonite clay and fiber to soften/break down mucoid plaque.

Bentonite clay is just as it sounds: it is grey-colored clay. Like a sponge, bentonite clay sucks up and absorbs everything the clay comes into contact with. Bentonite clay is what will grab the mucoid plaque, and pull it out of the lower intestines after being softened/broken down by the cleansing herbs.

Note: Bentonite clay is very powerful, sticky and glue-like. The bentonite must be combined together with psyllium husk fiber. The clay will absorb everything it encounters, and I mean everything. The bentonite clay can suck up the cleansing herb if taken together. Consume the cleansing herbs and the bentonite clay at least 1 hour–1.5 hours apart.

Fiber and cascara sagrada bark is what will forcefully pushes out the mucoid plaque from the bowels.

The cleansing herbs have the exact opposite effect of bentonite clay. Each of the cleansing herbs function differently during the cleanse.

Cleansing herbs:

Here I listed the supplements that work best.

Cascara sagrada bark is an absolute must. The more cleansing herbs taken, the faster and more effective the cleansing process will go

What does "take 5 drops" mean?

Take 5 drops every 1.5 hours together with cleansing herbs.

✓ **Plantain:** Best at breaking and softening mucoid plaque.

(take 5 drops together with the cleansing herbs)

Herb Pharm, Plantain, Fresh Leaf, 1 fl oz (30 ml) **$12.50**

✓ **Rhubarb Root:** Highly effective in breaking down mucoid plaque.

(drink together with the cleansing herbs)

Yogi Tea, Berry DeTox, Caffeine Free, 16 Tea Bags, 1.12 oz (32 g) **$5.85**

This tea tastes delicious and contains many detoxifying herbs.

(drink together with the cleansing herbs)

Yogi Tea, Detox, Caffeine Free, 16 Tea Bags, 1.02 oz (29 g) **$7.99**

✓ **Golden Echinacea:** Purifies the blood and destroys mucoid plaque.

(take 15 - 20 drops together with the cleansing herbs)

Nature's Way, Echinacea Goldenseal, Alcohol Free 99.9%, 1 fl oz (30 ml) **$7.59**

✓ **Barberry Root Bark:** Blood purifier, intestinal cleanser and eliminates bowel mucus.

This herb carries many detoxifying herbs.

(take 2-3 caps together with the cleansing herbs)

Nature's Way, Red Clover Blossom, 400 mg, 100 Veggie Caps **$7.04**

✓ **Licorice:** Improves blood circulation and destroys mucus.

(take 15 - 20 drops together with the cleansing herbs)

Nature's Answer, Licorice, Alcohol Free, 2,000 mg, 1 fl oz (30 ml) **9.25**

✓ **Digestive enzymes:** Breaks up and softens mucoid plaque + fires up digestion.

(take 2-3 caps together with the cleansing herbs)

Garden of Life, O-Zyme, Digestive Enzyme Blend, 90 Vegetarian Caplets **$28.99**

Garden of Life, Omega-Zyme, Digestive Enzyme Blend, 180 Veggie Caplets **$44.09**

✓ **Lobelia:** Improves elimination and mucoid plaque congestion.

(take 4-6 drops with cleansing herbs)

Herb Pharm Certified Organic Lobelia Extract - 1 oz **$10.56**

✓ **Cascara sagrada bark:** A powerful laxative herb that will push out the mucoid plaque once grasped by bentonite clay.

(take 1- 3 capsules… together with the cleansing herbs)

Nature's Way, Cascara Sagrada, Aged Bark, 180 Vcaps **$8.85**

Mucoid Plaque-Grabbing herbs:

Fibers are crucial to keep the secretion moving out of the bowels. Never allow the gunk to get stuck within during the cleanse. Plaque and all else must be expelled effectively, and quickly during the cleanse

✓ **Psyllium husk fiber:** Fiber is like a vacuum cleaner, absorbing all toxins and cleaning up mucoid plaque and outdated foods in the GI tract's path.(take 1 tablespoon together with bentonite clay)

Now Foods Psyllium Husk Powder, 24 oz **$15.29**

Yerba Prima, Psyllium Whole Husks, Colon Cleanser, 12 oz (340 g) **$11.36**

✓ **Bentonite clay:** Clay that grabs mucoid plaque

(take 1 tablespoon together with fiber)

Yerba Prima, Great Plains, Bentonite, Detox, 32 fl oz **$15.95**

✓ During stage 1, drink as much water + unlimited green drinks throughout the day, eating 2- 3 large meals of raw vegetables, and every 1.5–2 hours take the necessary herbs and supplements.

Note: The cascara sagrada bark is a strong laxative. It's sufficient for me to consume 1-2 capsules every 1.5 hours. The key is to pay attention to your stools (poop). Your stools must be solid and loose, but not liquid diarrhea or runny. If by taking 2 cascara sagrada capsules causes your stools to be runny, then cut back to 1 cap. Or take an extra dose of bentonite clay with fiber. Listen to your body and control the herbs accordingly. Remember to consume the bentonite clay at least 1 hour to 1.5 hours apart from the cleansing herbs because the bentonite clay will suck up all the herbs. At the same time, if your bowel movements become too slow, take more cascara sagrada and fiber. Experiment with the doses.

The mucoid plaque will expel out of your system mixed in your stools (poop). Mucoid plaque can look green, grey, or even black...the texture of mucoid plaque can be rubbery, clay-like, or thick and hard like asphalt. You will be able to distinguish between your regular stools and mucoid plaque. Again, do some image searches on mucoid plaque.

You should have several bowel movements (5 - 8 times) a day during stage 1 and 2 of the cleanse.

Use common sense to adjust to the cleanse the best way it fits your schedule.

Here is a sample of stage 1 cleansing day:

7:00 am: In the morning, take cleansing herbs (3 enzyme caps + 1 cascara cap + 5 drops of plantain + 2 lobelia cap + Rhubarb root tea + 15 drops of golden Echinacea + 2 caps of Barberry Root Bark + 15 drops of Licorice + 1 teaspoon of green drink powder + glass of water); drink plenty of green drinks.

8:30 am: 1.5 hours later, consume (1 tablespoon of bentonite clay + 1 tablespoon of fiber + 1 teaspoon of green drink powder + glass of water).

9:00: Eat raw vegetables.

10:00 am: Take cleansing herbs with green drinks.

11:30 am: Consume bentonite clay + fiber + together with green drinks.

1:00 pm: Take cleansing herbs with green drinks.

2:30 pm: Consume bentonite clay + fiber + together with green drinks.

4:00 pm: Take cleansing herbs with green drinks.

5:30 pm: Eat raw vegetables.

7:00 pm: Consume bentonite clay + fiber + together with green drinks.

8:30 pm: Take cleansing herbs with green drinks.

10:00 pm: Consume bentonite clay + fiber + together with green drinks.

11:00 pm: Before going to sleep, take probiotics (transplanting friendly bacteria in later pages).

Stay on stage 1 for 3-4 days. Listen to your body. Keep in mind the cleansing reactions. If the cleansing reactions become too strong, end the cleanse here. If you feel like your body can handle more, go to the next stage after a couple of days.

Stage 1 (2 – 4 days)   Stage 2 (3 – 4 days)   (stage 1 + 2 = total of 6 - 8 days)

Stage 2 is the final and vigorous stage. You will be doing everything the same as stage 1; the only difference is that you will not eat any solid foods...nothing solid whatsoever!

During this stage, you will be drinking unlimited amounts of green drinks. The more alkalizing vegetable juices, the more cleansing. Since you will not be eating any solid foods for a few days, whenever you lack energy, consume coconut oil, flax oil, and cod liver oil. You have to be strong... this is the stage where most of the mucoid plaque will be expelled from your system.

Here is a sample of a stage 2 cleansing day:

7:00 am: In the morning, take cleansing herbs (3 enzyme caps + 1 cascara cap + 5 drops of plantain + 2 lobelia cap + Rhubarb root tea + 15 drops of golden Echinacea + 2 caps of Barberry Root Bark + 15 drops of Licorice + 1 teaspoon of green drink powder + glass of water); drink plenty of green drinks.

8:30 am: 1.5 hours, later consume (1 tablespoon of bentonite clay + 1 tablespoon of fiber + 1 teaspoon of green drink powder + water).

10:00 am: Take cleansing herbs with green drinks.

11:30 am: Consume bentonite clay + fiber + together with green drinks.

1:00 pm: Take cleansing herbs with green drinks.

2:30 pm: Consume bentonite clay + fiber + together with green drinks.

4:00 pm: Take cleansing herbs with green drinks.

5:30 pm: Consume bentonite clay + fiber + together with green drinks.

7:00 pm: Take cleansing herbs with green drinks.

9:30 pm: Consume bentonite clay + fiber + together with green drinks.

11:00 pm: Before going to sleep, consume probiotics. (transplanting friendly bacteria in later pages)

Stay on stage 2 for 3 - 4 days. Listen to your body. Keep in mind the cleansing reactions.

Note: The max length I was on the cleanse was 7 days. You could stay on the cleanse for longer; however, I would not recommend going over 10 days because the internal organ's peristaltic actions will weaken. If you absolutely feel like you can max out, stay on the cleanse for 15 days → **and slowly slide back into digestion over a period of several days.**

How to end the cleanse:

Ending the cleanse properly is extremely important. Your body was on a long fast. Pounds upon pounds (kilos and kilos) of bowel mucus, unfriendly bacteria, fungal overgrowth, parasites →a whole load of unnecessary gunk that had built up for years upon years has just been removed in only a few short days. It is vitally important  to not shock your system all of a sudden by eating heavy meals immediately after a cleanse. Soothe back into digestion by first consuming easily digestible foods as vegetable soups, miso soup, some cooked/raw vegetables and fruits. Slowly facilitate back into eating ordinarily in the course of 2 -3 days.

What happens after a cleanse?

One cleanse alone will not eliminate completely all the mucoid plaque and toxicity buildup in the intestines over decades. Several cleanses are necessary to commence. However, every deep internal cleanse leaves the organs weakened. You must re-construct/re-strengthen and transplant friendly bacteria **after every cleanse**. In the beginning, I suggest doing a major cleanse during the spring and in the following fall.

If you would like to do back to back cleanses, you can. Just make sure to stay on the bowel regeneration phase for a couple of weeks before beginning a new cleanse. Chronically cleansing alone will cause more damage than good.

Deep tissue cleansing during the summer is fine, only avoid the cold winters. From then onwards, do one major 6 – 7-day cleanse once a year during the spring.

Pro cleanser:

Once you become proficient at cleansing, skip directly to stage 2. Start and end the cleanse with stage 2.

Eradicate Parasites, Fungi, Molds and Candida Overgrowth:

You cannot know without looking inside your body using dark field microscopy (live blood cell analysis), iridology, or kinesiology if you carry fungal overgrowth or have parasites. Most likely everyone has contracted some form of mold and parasites at one point or another, but to be 100% sure, you require accurate feedback.

A good way to find out would be to take the herbs, and perceive the die-off reactions your body produces.

A deep internal detoxification would have gotten rid of most 80% - 90% of the internal molds and parasites. In cases of severe fungal overgrowth and parasites, you will have to eradicate using the following methods.

Note: The bowel lining cannot be effectively reconstructed unless parasites and fungal overgrowth are thoroughly dead and intestines are flourishing with friendly bacteria.

Note: The parasite and fungal herbs have to be taken DURING the cleanse together with the cleansing herbs.

Parasites:

There can be over 100+ different kinds of parasites living, breathing and feeding off your nutrients inside of your body. From tapeworms that are several inches in length to tiny microbes, parasites can be stuck in many if not all the body's organs.

Parasites live in dirty, unclean environments. And as long as your system is not cleaned out and in an alkaline state, parasites will always be a problem. These insects/worms/or bugs can be contracted by eating meats, dirty meats and drinking/eating unclean foods. Like a flea on a dog, parasites steal our nutrients from within.

Keep in mind that killing parasites produces a die-off effect. The die-off reactions can be brutal. You can take the parasite herbs and judge if you have parasites by the die-off effects.

✓ **Black Walnut Hull Tincture** (take 10 drops 1st day… increase by 2 drops for 6 days)

Nature's Answer, Black Walnut & Wormwood, Alcohol-Free, 2,000 mg, 1 fl oz (30 ml)
$11.35

Experiment with the doses according to how your body responds.

The best way to get rid of parasites is by avoiding them. Parasites feed on sugar, white flour and animal meat. An alkaline internal environment and proper doses of the right fats will keep these awful insects away.

33

Fungal overgrowth:

To prevent molds and fungi from growing inside the system, it is not sufficient to only eradicate the fungi but to maintain a clean and alkaline environment within the bowels. If you have read the weight loss or bodybuilding texts, you will know exactly how to do this.

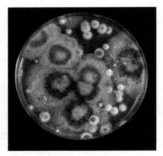

All life forms have one purpose of existing... and that is to survive. Molds cannot survive in a clean and alkaline environment. If your system becomes acidic, molds will re-grow. That is why keeping an alkaline internal system is crucial to health.

Fungi pollute and stress all the other organs, especially the liver.

All types of fungal overgrowth must be eradicated. Oil of oregano will wipe out every kind of mold inside the body. **If you choose this route... kill all the molds on the bowel cleansing phase several hours apart from transplanting friendly bacteria. For example, kill parasites in the morning, take the probiotics during the night.**

Oil of oregano: (take 5- 10 drops day until molds are completely gone)

Natural Factors, Oil of Oregano, 1 fl oz (30 ml) **$18.50**

Eradicating molds discharges the most severe die-off reaction of all die-off reactions. The first time I took antifungal agents, I felt very sick. The die-off reaction lasted for a good couple minutes. I collapsed on my bed unable to get back up for about 5 minutes.

You have to listen to your body. In the beginning, the die-off reactions will be severe, but they gradually diminish until they are non-existent. Listen to your body, and eradicate all fungal overgrowth completely in order to successfully reconstruct your bowel lining. Again, this is not possible without any kind of refined method of looking inside. Experiment with the doses until the molds are gone.

To fully reconstruct the bowel lining, fungi and parasites must be completely eradicated. A deep internal bowel cleanse will have gotten rid of 80% - 90% of parasites and molds. And friendly bacteria will fight off molds in the long-term.

TRANSPLANT FRIENDLY BACTERIA:

Absorption of nutrients occurs in the small and large intestinal walls. Friendly bacteria maintain the colon at proper pH levels, prevents fungal growth, and assimilates nutrition.

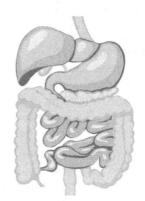

The bowels must flourish with friendly bacteria known as probiotics, or else assimilation of nutrition from foods and supplements will go to waste.

How are friendly bacteria transplanted into the bowels?

- Bowels cannot be acidic

- Bowels must be alkaline

- Cannot be on antibiotics (worst enemy of probiotics that will wipe out friendly intestinal flora entirely)

Note: The best time to transplant probiotics is during/after a deep internal detoxification.

If you're following the diet as outlined in the "what to eat" section, your bowels should be free of acidity, be alkaline, and be ready to transplant intestinal flora.

However, this isn't the entire battle. Think of transplanting friendly bacteria as a war. Currently, unfriendly bacteria have colonized the land (small intestines, large intestines) and it must be re-colonized by friendly bacteria. For the friendly army to successfully colonize the bowels, a large and powerful army must be sent to the battlefront to completely replace the non-friendly bacteria army.

Most probiotic supplements made of acidophilus will die off shortly after consumption inside the stomach before it can reach the intestines. Probiotics are very fragile, and most probiotic supplements do not implant at all or die fairly rapidly.

Lactobifudus and streptococcus are what implant for long periods of time most effortlessly.

Here's the best probiotic that contains lactobifudus and streptococcus, stay alive and flourish inside the bowels for months at a time.

Garden of Life, Primal Defense, HSO Probiotic Formula, 90 Veggie Caplets **$26.49**

Garden of Life, Primal Defense, HSO Probiotic Formula, 216 Caplets **$51.90**

Consume 6 or more caplets with lots of water and fiber in the morning or evening on an empty stomach for at least 3 weeks or longer. Don't be afraid to experiment. Remember, think of colonizing friendly bacteria as an army would invade enemy grounds.

To keep your bowels fully colonized, have a transplant session every 6 months. A superb method to keep friendly bacteria alive is by taking kefir daily. (check out Monstrous and Detox programs)

Inulin (FOS)

As you have learned, probiotics are very fragile, and they need their own source of food to flourish. Then special fiber feeds friendly bacteria. However, the average fiber supplements won't be sufficient. There is a special fiber by the name of fructooligosaccharides (FOS), also known as inulin, causes insane overgrowth of the intestinal flora.

Add some inulin stevia to your drinks or foods. Here are two of my favorite inulin stevia products that come in powder form. Again, experiment with the stevia doses and products.

Now Foods, Better Stevia Balance, Zero Calories, 100 Packets, (1.1 g) Each **$10.35**

Now Foods, Organic, BetterStevia, Zero Calorie Sweetener, 75 Packets, 2.65 oz (75 g)
$5.60

Goat Milk and Tibetan Kefir Mushrooms:

What KIND of milk harms or doesn't harm the bones?

Milk in its natural form is raw milk, and is put in the category of alkaline drinks. The milk 99% of people drink, bought from the supermarket that has been pasteurized and homogenized, is acidic.

Unpasteurized, non- homogenized milk is the milk that provides all the nutrients to the bones and body. Pasteurized milk found in the grocery stores and supermarkets has been heated to kill bacteria. This is the milk which harms the bones, causes allergens, etc.

Cow milk is extremely difficult for the stomach to digest. And in many cases, causes inflammation. Cows have four stomachs that function nothing like a human's. Cow milk and all dairy processed dairy products from the grocery store simply is inconsumable.

Know that there is a healthier alternative for cow milk. Goat milk is packed with nutrients- copper, zinc, magnesium, calcium, vitamins- A, B2, C, D, and tastes pretty much the same as cow milk.

Goat milk carries A2 protein, which is the closest to human breast milk. Goat milk is easy to digest, lower in lactose, doesn't carry the allergens cow milk contains, and is low in casein protein. Protein congests the system and is hard to digest. The casein protein in cow milk causes allergies, inflammations, and supports bowel irritations, leaky gut syndrome, and a whole lot of gastrointestinal issues. High levels of medium-chain fatty acids found in goat milk converts to energy instead of storing as excess body fat.

Where can raw, unpasteurized, non-homogenized goat's milk be purchased?

Finding raw goat milk can be extremely difficult. But once you find a quality supplier, the supply of goat milk will be well worth the effort.

Raw goat milk won't be available in any kind of supermarket or grocery store. Depending in which country you live in, the best way to find raw goat's milk is to do an internet search. If you cannot find it on the internet, you will most likely have to contact a dairy company/factory directly, and if that doesn't work, go to a farm with goats, and ask for some raw milk.

Where can Tibetan Kefir Mushrooms be purchase?

Kefir mushrooms are fairly easy to find and cost effective.

The same deal here as goat milk: Depending where you live, you will have to search the internet. Kefir grains are living organisms. All you have to do is purchase the grains once, re-supply the goat milk and the grains will multiply over time.

How to make kefir:

Making kefir mixed with goat milk is a straight forward process.

Necessary tools:

- Plastic strainer.

- Plastic spoon.

- Glass jar (traditional milk pint bottle size) with holes punctured on the lid for oxygen.

Leave the remainder of the unused goat milk refrigerated.

Pour enough goat milk to fill up 1/3 of the bottle. Place the kefir grains inside to blend with the milk. Allow the kefir to

fuse with the milk for 24 hours at room temperature. The kefir granules will prevent the milk from rotting. You will know what I mean.

24 hours later....

The milk should have become thick, sludge-like and, the kefir granules will float up to the surface. Separate the kefir grains from the milk by pouring the mixture into a container, filtered by a plastic strainer.

Note: The kefir grains are fragile living organisms. Avoid touching with a metallic object or with fingers.

Place the kefir granules aside. In the plastic strainer, gently rinse the kefir mushrooms with water. Prepare a new kefir mixture to leave for 24 hours. Notice that the kefir granules have multiplied.

Time to drink the kefir infused milk. Goat milk alone tastes delicious. Kefir mixed with goat milk left for 24 hours in room temperature tastes quite horrible. The taste is sour, and smells awful. I like to mix some slices of bananas, and flavored stevia with the kefir drink. If the taste is still intolerable, mix some cocoa together with flavored stevia.

Remember, taste comes last.

Search some videos online on how to make kefir.

Drink kefir mixed with goat milk once or twice a day, permanently. The kefir fused with goat milk will multiply the existing probiotics from the primal defense tablets, and continuously add more and regenerate probiotics in the bowels forever.

RECONSTRUCTION OF THE INTESTINAL WALLS

Over years eating harmful foods, such as gluten grains, sugar, and white flour, not only amass kilos of mucoid plaque, but the bowel lining becomes severely damaged. The intestinal walls can be punctured by hundreds if not thousands of holes known as leaky gut syndrome. Through these holes, food particles can leak out causing allergies, slowing down bowel movement, stressing neighboring organs and placing a heavy burden on the gallbladder, stomach, and liver.

You have just cleaned out a large portion of mucoid plaque was attached to the intestinal walls. You are 50% done. Another factor to consider is that deep internal tissue cleansing puts a lot of stress on the body, which leaves the organs weakened. And if that is not enough, you have to fix the intestinal walls until they no longer leak. Once leaky gut syndrome has been fixed and intestines re-strengthened, bowel movements will be large and old digested food will be eliminated quickly.

Note: Once leaky gut has been cured, by eating the wrong foods as coffee, or large quantities of white flour, leaky gut will return.

How can these punctured holes be fixed?

Believe it or not, the human body has the ability to reconstruct/regenerate and re-strengthen intestinal lining like a salamander is able to grow a new tail. Humans cannot re-grow an arm or a leg, but we can reconstruct or manufacture our delicate intestinal lining. Pretty interesting, isn't it?

First you have to take the stress off the intestines during the reconstruction process. White flour and refined white flour products become difficult to digest and sticky inside the body. Wheat, spelt, rye → all types of grain → and coffee upset intestinal lining the most. Reduce the consumption of these foods during the reconstruction phase. It would be wise to cut out all white flour, coffee and grain products temporarily until leaky gut has been completely fixed. To fully understand how to prevent mucoid plaque buildup, check out my other programs:

1. *How to Burn Body Fat Completely and Maintain a Slim Physique Permanently*

2. *How to Build More Muscle than Ever Before and Maintain Muscle Mass Permanently*

Everything from what causes leaky gut, mucoid plaque buildup, fat accumulation, source of fuel for the body, acidic vs alkaline, etc., is covered in these 2 programs.

Second, consume psyllium husk fiber, green drinks and high fiber/easily digestible raw vegetables daily. Again, all of this is covered in my other programs.

HOW TO RECONSTRUCT THE INTESTINAL WALL:

There are different types of foods and supplementation that works synergistically to successfully reconstruct delicate bowel lining. The inner body tissue of the aloe plant stimulates the healing procedure. L-glutamine and amino acids from pre-digested white fish are amino acids that provide the basic building blocks to patch the leaky gut holes and reconstruct the delicate intestinal lining.

Note: In my experience, L-glutamine was all that was necessary to heal my leaky gut syndrome. But if you do not experience results with L-glutamine, switch over to amino acids from white fish.

Take l-glutamine or the seacure products. If you can, take both. Don't be surprised if you suddenly gain more muscle mass after the cleanse.

✓ **L- glutamine:** provides the basic building blocks

(take 1 teaspoon…3 times a day)

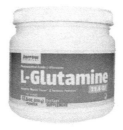

Jarrow Formulas L-Glutamine, 17.6 Oz **$21.99**

✓ **Amino acid from white fish:** provides the basic building blocks

(take 2- 3 caps…3 times a day)

Seacure 180 Hydrolized White Fish Blister Packs **$36.98**

Seacure 180 Capsules **$35.73**

How to eat the aloe plant:

The best method is to cut the hardened green skin off the aloe pant and eat the inner body tissue. Eat as much aloe as possible→ one large aloe plant per day, to several pounds or more. Aloe in green drinks is easy to digest and alkalizing. If you don't have access to aloe plants, the same results can be achieved with aloe supplements. One more tip: unrefined coconut oil helps the regeneration process. Be sure to take unrefined coconut oil during this time.

✓ **Aloe supplementation:** heals delicate intestinal lining

(take 1- 2 capsule…3 times a day)

manapol powder

Nature's Herbs, Aloe Vera, Inner Leaf, 100 Veggie Caps **$12.97**

The manapol powder works much better than the aloe herbs. You will have to purchase the manapol powder directly from their website.

In order of best results.

1st. Natural aloe plant

2nd. Manapol

3rd. Aloe herbs

How long to be on the intestinal reconstruction phase:

As you have learned, if the intestinal walls are damaged, bowel transit time will be slow and food particles will leak. You have to stay on the reconstruction phase until the bowels don't leak any longer and bowel movements come nice and easy.

Note: One intestinal cleanse won't rid all the mucoid plaque buildup you have accumulated during your entire life. More than one cleanse is needed. When and how to cleanse is listed above.

KEEP IN MIND after every cleanse, re-transplanting friendly bacteria and intestinal reconstruction is absolutely required. If you only cleanse, the internal organs will be weakened and prone to unfriendly bacteria accumulation.

ALSO KEEP IN MIND to rest a 1-2 of weeks after a cleanse. Chronically cleansing without rest is counterproductive. Listen to your body; if you feel like you can begin another internal detoxification session, by all means do so. Make sure you rest in between cleanse sessions.

How to know if the intestinal walls are leaking:

Listen to your body...

✓ Stools (poop) with a powerful offensive odor means intestinal toxemia.

✓ Unformed and loose stools mean leaky gut.

✓ Bits and pieces on undigested food particles signifies the need to chew your food more thoroughly, and/or you may have leaky gut.

✓ Less than 2- 3 bowels movements a day means slow bowels in need of cleansing and/or stay on the reconstruction phase.

Healthy stools are well formed, large, thick and shaped like the intestines. You should have a bowel movement shortly after awakening, and 30- 40 minutes after every significant meal. The pre-digested meal will be removed quickly for a new digestion cycle to begin. You should have 3 bowel movements or more per day and need little toilet paper.

Stay on the reconstruction phase for 2 - 4 weeks to a couple of months until the bowels stop leaking.

Other approaches to know what is going on in the system:

Tongue:

Go to the mirror and stick out your tongue. Pay attention to the color of your tongue's surface. If there's a thick white coating on the tongue, this can mean 3 things...

1. Weak digestion.

2. Intestines are full of mucoid plaque.

3. Fungal overgrowth.

Or a combination of 2 or all the above. The thicker the white coating, the more a deep internal cleanse is necessary.

Iridology:

Iridology Chart

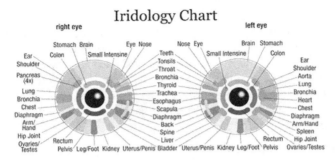

Iridology is the science of studying the iris to see what is going on inside the body. I have visited an iridologist and they have pinned down leaky gut, coffee addiction, poor digestion, fungal overgrowth, lack of probiotics and so much more that was going wrong in my body.

The iridologist will take a picture of your iris, and can know everything that is going wrong inside the body.

CONCLUSION:

I hope you have gained some new enlightened information by reading this program. I have cleansed and reconstructed my intestines over and over in the past few years. Believe me, knowing how to properly cleanse and reconstruct your bowels will reward your body for the rest of your life. Reading alone will never deliver results. You will have to act on what you learn to benefit from and experience results.

Thank you and good luck on the cleanse(s)!

As an author, I value your reviews. It helps others to make an informed decision before reading the book. If you feel you have gained enlightened knowledge, please consider leaving a short review in the following link.

It'd be greatly appreciated!

www.nekoterran.com/advice

If you have not signed up for my weight loss or bodybuilding newsletter, feel free to sign up using the link below to receive more valuable advice on health and fitness from me.

BONUS #2: *(Absolutely a must to achieve top shape)* Sign up to receive the BEST home bodyweight workout and more health advice from me.

www.nekoterran.com/advice

All Titles B&W and Color

available at CreateSpace Store...

To learn <u>more</u> go to

www.Nekoterran.com

More Health & Fitness Titles:

Basic Bodybuilding

- ✓ What builds muscles.
- ✓ What causes muscle mass deterioration.
- ✓ What causes body fat.
- ✓ How to burn body fat.
- ✓ How to maintain muscle mass.
- ✓ How to maintain a fat-less physique.
- ✓ *Choose only basic bodybuilding or basic weight loss.*

Basic Weight Loss

- ✓ What tones/strengthens muscles.
- ✓ What causes muscle mass deterioration.
- ✓ What causes body fat.
- ✓ How to prevent body fat.
- ✓ How to burn existing body fat.
- ✓ How to maintain muscle mass.
- ✓ How to maintain a fat-less physique.
- ✓ *Choose only basic bodybuilding or basic weight loss.*

Choose only **one** program – Weight Loss or Bodybuilding

Basic Internal Detox

- ✓ Deep internal detoxification program.
- ✓ This is the ideal program to begin with.
- ✓ Complete this program first before attempting weight loss or bodybuilding basics
- ✓ *Works in conjunction with every other program.*

Advanced Bodybuilding

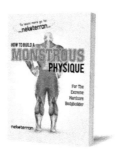

- ✓ For the advanced bodybuilder.
- ✓ The final step out of 3.
- ✓ *Must first complete the internal detox program.*
- ✓ *Must first complete the basic bodybuilding program.*

CPSIA information can be obtained
at www.ICGtesting.com
Printed in the USA
BVHW041951010419
544269BV00016B/221/P